BUILDING BROOKLYN BRIDGE

BUILDING
BROOKLYN BRIDGE

by F. Wenderoth Saunders

Illustrated by the Author

LITTLE, BROWN AND COMPANY
Boston · Toronto

Books written and illustrated by F. Wenderoth Saunders

CROSSROADS OF CONQUERORS

BUILDING BROOKLYN BRIDGE

Illustrated by F. Wenderoth Saunders

MY FIRST GEOGRAPHY OF THE PANAMA CANAL

by Arensa Sondergaard

BUILDING BROOKLYN BRIDGE

With its feet wide apart and planted firmly in the water, Brooklyn Bridge every day supports on arms of steel and wire thousands of people crossing the East River from Brooklyn and New York. Brooklyn Bridge was the first of a great race of giants long enough and high enough for ocean liners to pass beneath them. The Bridge has been praised in poetry and in pictures because it brought freedom of movement to the millions who live in Brooklyn and the rest of Long Island, because it is the grandfather of great suspension bridges for millions of people in other parts of the world, and because to many it is the most graceful and beautiful of all bridges. It has fired men's imagi-

nations, and they have called it one of the seven wonders of the world.

You can see children of the grandfather bridge over the East River, spanning the Hudson River, at the Straits of Mackinac, at San Francisco, at Lisbon in Portugal, across the Narrows from New York to Staten Island, and at many other places. But this was not always so!

From the time the Dutch came to New York, engineers said that no bridge could be built across the East River because that body of water — which is not a river at all, but a salt water strait — was too wide and the ocean tides surging in it were too treacherous. No bridge could last, they said; its piers would shift in the oozy mud and the bridge would fall. Yet everyone was eager to have a bridge. Even the engineers who laughed at the idea wanted it, but they all wished for it the way some people wish for a million dollars, knowing that their wish would never come true.

Long before there were any big bridges into New York, Brooklyn itself was a big city from which thousands of persons crossed the East River daily to go to work. These people had to depend on ferries. They crowded themselves and their horses and carts on the double-ended boats which huffed their way from shore to shore. A crossing by ferry was pleasant enough in the hot summer, because the cool ocean breezes swept up the river, and the gulls circling over the sailing ships and steamers made passengers in the ferries feel as if they too might be coming from India or China or the ends of the earth.

Crossing in the middle of winter, on the other hand, if you could cross at all, was sometimes a terrible and even dangerous experience. Winters used to be colder than they are now. There were times when the East River, despite all the salt water in it, froze solid from bank to bank, and people walked

across. And there were other times when the East
River was choked with great chunks of ice because a
sudden thaw had enabled the tides to break up the
solid surface.

On just such a day, riding on a ferry, an engineer
got the idea that a suspension bridge could be built
over the East River. And this engineer, John Augustus
Roebling, told himself that he was the man to do it.

That day it took the ferry several hours to make
the crossing. Black smoke belching from its stacks and
paddle wheels churning, it bravely bucked the ice
floes. Its captain flirted with danger by turning and
twisting the ferryboat among the icy pieces of the jig-
saw puzzle, but often the drifting floes would close in
to grind and bump against paddle wheels and hull.
For minutes the ferry would make no headway. Passengers, muffled in their overcoats, huddled against
the steam pipes in the cabins. Horses hitched to drays,
wagons and carriages shivered under their blankets

while their half-frozen masters cursed the wind that numbed them through and through.

During the long hours of that passage only John Augustus Roebling seemed unaffected by the cold.

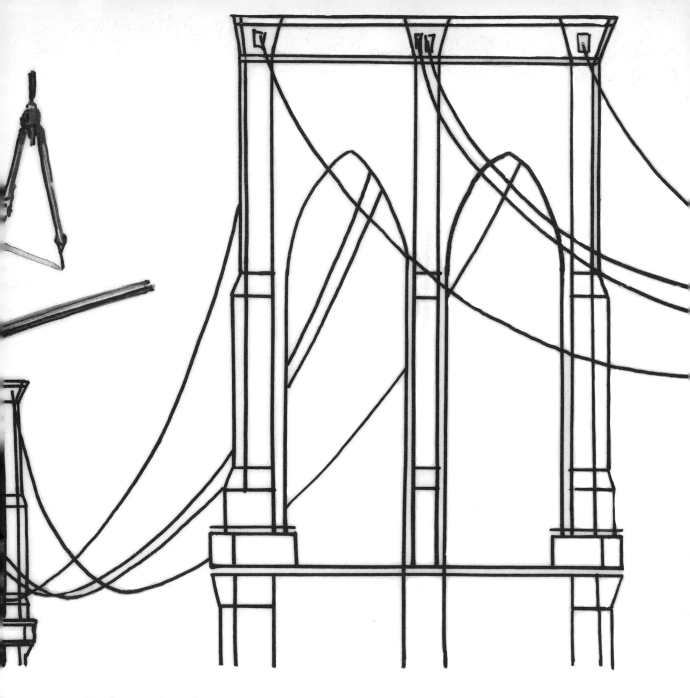

Before the ferry reached the other shore he saw the
shape of the bridge in his mind. Two beautiful towers
reached skyward like the towers of a cathedral. From
these towers hung festoons of steel cable to support

13

the spans stretching from New York to Brooklyn.

The idea of the suspension bridge was not new at this time. Roebling had built several; in fact he had brought the type nearly to perfection. But nothing of a size to span the East River had been attempted. By comparison the towers and cables for a bridge to Brooklyn would have to be gigantic. Nevertheless, Roebling was certain it could be done successfully. He drew up preliminary plans and persuaded business-men to put up the money to build the bridge. Un-fortunately he did not live to see the great day when his bridge was opened.

The building of the bridge-giant was a mighty task. The East River was a formidable foe which

14

proved more than once the truth of the saying from ancient times, "To build a bridge requires a life!" The first man to die was Roebling.

As John Roebling stood on the edge of the Fulton Street Ferry Slip sighting the exact location for the Brooklyn tower, he failed to notice a ferry easing into its berth. The ferry pushed against a rack designed to break the momentum of the boat. The rack in turn pushed against the piling where Roebling was standing, catching one of his feet and crushing it. Carried to his son's home in Brooklyn, John Roebling died two weeks later of blood poisoning.

Fortunately a father has never had a son better fitted to carry on his work. Trained for years to be his father's assistant, Washington Roebling was a graduate of Stevens Institute of Technology. As a colonel of engineers in the Civil War he had surmounted many kinds of difficulty. Colonel Roebling was selected immediately by the bridge backers to carry on his father's plans, which were drawn up and waiting.

Constructing any big bridge is a tremendous job, usually complicated by unexpected problems. But to erect a huge suspension bridge with untried methods and materials was a true labor of Hercules. The great towers which would support the cables could not stand on mud, shifting sand or quicksand. Such high towers would tumble quickly without a firm base. Colonel Roebling was a resourceful man. He thought he knew a way to push the mud and sand to one side to reach the rock underneath. On this rock he would build the solid piers of the towers, the giant's legs.

A few months before his father's death, Colonel Roebling had returned from Europe, where he had gone to study a new invention called a caisson. The idea of the caisson is simple. If you make a box with watertight sides and top, leave the bottom open, and press the box down through the water to the bed of a stream, you have a caisson. An air hose through the

top carries compressed air into the caisson to force the water out through a pipe in the roof and keep water from pouring in where the bottom edges of the caisson rest on the river bottom. In this watertight shell

THE BROOKLYN CAISSON

A CUTAWAY SHOWING THE TYPES OF EQUIPMENT USED

THERE WERE TWO ENTRANCE SHAFTS, TWO SUPPLY SHAFTS, TWO SHAFTS TO BRING UP MATERIAL DUG OR BLASTED FROM THE RIVER BOTTOM, SIX AIR COMPRESSOR PUMPS AND MANY PIPES FOR BLOWING OUT SAND AND FOR FURNISHING GAS AND WATER.

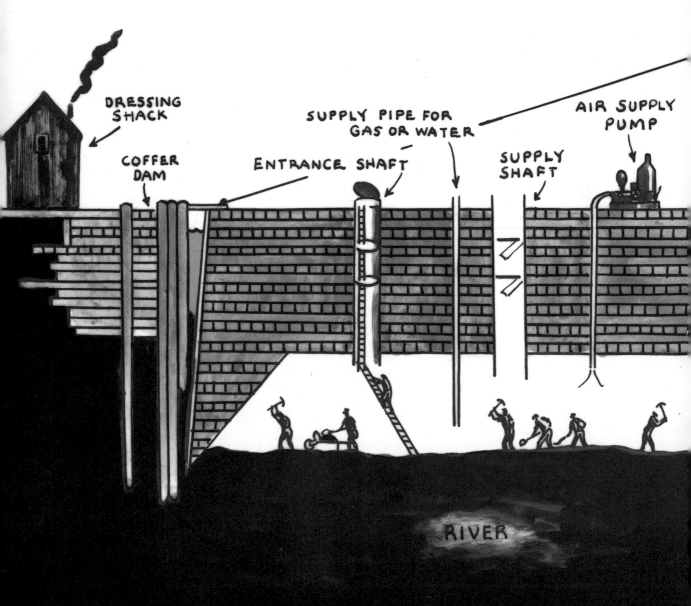

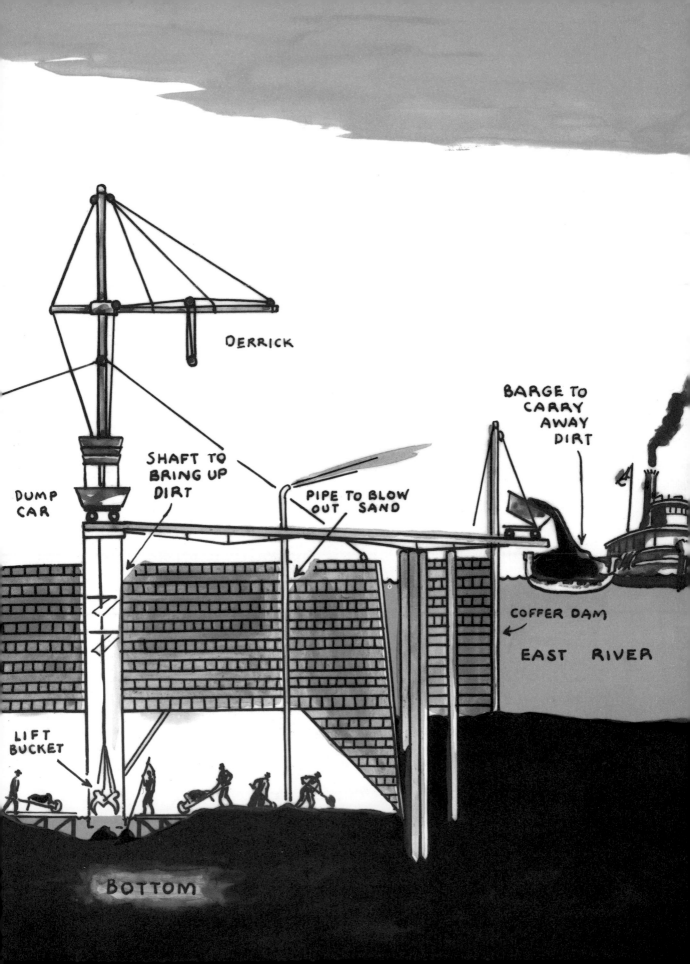

men can work on the bottom digging away mud and sand.

However, such a big caisson would be needed to make solid footing for the giant bridge that no one knew whether it would work or not. Could men inside it stand the greatly increased air pressure needed to keep the water out? The pressure would have to be increased constantly as the caisson settled lower and lower.

Colonel Roebling was confident that the caisson could be used successfully. In 1869, the year that real work on the bridge started, he had the caisson built at a shipyard in Brooklyn. The caisson was so big that it spread out over seven marine railways. A marine railway is like a wide railroad track on which a ship is built. When the ship is launched, it glides down the track into the water.

Roebling's caisson was larger than seven clipper ships built side by side! Certainly it was the strangest ship ever launched in the old shipyard. The carpenters had built the sidewalls like wooden wedges, nine feet thick at the top tapering down till at the open bottom they were practically cutting edges. The outside and the bottom edge were covered with steel

plates, and the top or roof was made of heavy timbers fifteen feet thick.

Once in place Colonel Roebling's caisson would be filled with concrete to become the giant's foot, the foundation for the tower that would rise more than 300 feet in the air. The wooden part of the caisson, since the air could not reach it, would stay sound and strong for hundreds of years.

Divers had determined that less mud and sand would have to be dug away on the Brooklyn side to reach the rock, so six tugboats towed the caisson to the prepared site on that side. Compressed air kept the caisson barely afloat until it was in position, where it was allowed to settle to the bottom with its top still above water.

Before work started inside the caisson, derricks were raised on its top, schooners brought loads of dressed granite from New England quarries, and three shifts of stonemasons worked round the clock laying courses of masonry that weighted the caisson firmly down. To keep themselves above water the stone-

masons had to build at least as fast as the caisson settled.

Six wrought-iron shafts went down through the top of the caisson into the working chamber, which was subdivided into fourteen room-like sections to strengthen the roof. Numerous pipes entered the caisson for supplying air, water and gas and as exits for blowing out sand. The two entrance shafts had chambers where air pressure could be increased or decreased to accustom the workmen to different air pressures. There were two shafts down which supplies could be lowered, and two other shafts by which excavated material could be sent to the surface.

In each of the excavation shafts was a dredge bucket that opened on the bottom like a great jaw with a set of teeth. At the bases of these shafts were open wells of water where the workmen could dump wheelbarrow loads of sand, mud and gravel for the

CUTAWAY PICTURE
SHOWING CAISSON
REACHING FINAL DEPTH
WHICH IS SOLID ROCK;
TOWER RISES FROM
STONE PLATFORM

RIVER
BOTTOM

AIR
LOCK

SHAFT TO
BRING UP
RIVER
BOTTOM

WOODEN
CAISSON

OUTER
METAL
COVERING

ROCK
BOTTOM

dredge bucket to pick up. All shafts through which supplies and excavated materials had to be passed were equipped with pressure chambers or air locks so that the great pressure in the caisson would not blow out.

Since no one knew whether or not the caisson was safe to enter, it took courage to go down into it the first time. Colonel Roebling would not ask any man to do what he would not do himself, so he and a volunteer were the first to enter the air lock or decompression chamber. An attendant shut the circular hatch cover over them and turned on the compressed air. The incoming air sounded like the rush of fast water, and for a few anxious moments the men thought their eardrums would burst, but the pain soon went. When a gauge showed that the pressure in the air lock equaled the pressure in the caisson, Roebling's companion removed a plate from the floor, revealing an iron ladder fastened to a side of the shaft. Down the ladder the two men descended to the river bottom. Soon they were followed by a crew of diggers who commenced work immediately.

In 1870 men still dug by hand shovel, and progress at the end of the first week was only six inches, with forty-four feet to go. The giant's foot was refusing to

28

CUTAWAY OF AN AIR LOCK IN THE ENTRANCE SHAFT.
BEFORE ONE COULD ENTER THE CAISSON, THE AIR PRES-
SURE IN THE LOCK HAD TO BE INCREASED UNTIL IT WAS
THE SAME AS THAT IN THE CAISSON. IN LEAVING, THE
PRESSURE IN THE AIR LOCK WAS DECREASED UNTIL IT WAS
THE SAME AS THAT OF THE OUTSIDE AIR.

go down. Boulders too big for the dredge buckets and hardpan defied the diggers. To speed up the work, Colonel Roebling thought of gunpowder to blow up the boulders and rocky patches, but no one had ever used explosives under greatly increased air pressure. He determined to find out what would happen. With

a whole arsenal of pistols of various sizes he went down into the caisson by himself to shoot off the fire-arms in succession, beginning with the smallest. Nothing dangerous happened. So he fired off larger and larger amounts of the new smokeless blasting powder. Success! The obstructions could be broken up by ex-

plosives. Work now went according to schedule. As the men dug, the caisson settled lower and lower.

One day soon after the experiment with the explosives the stonemasons working above on the tower were nearly frightened to death. The giant let out a frightful belch from under the water, shooting sand and stones in a great waterspout sixty feet into the air. The crew ran shrieking from the foundation, tumbling into barges and boats and jumping into the water in their haste to escape. What had happened was that as the caisson was settling, the inside air, whose pres-

sure was greater than that of the water, found an escape-hole under one of the side edges. No one was hurt, and the stonemasons soon grew accustomed to these occasional, unexpected eruptions.

Down, down, down went the caisson week by week. Above, the stonemasons kept pace, laying course after course. Then without warning from under the waters of the East River came the terrible cry of "FIRE!"

"Call Colonel Roebling!" men shouted. When Roebling entered the caisson, he found the roof timbers ablaze. If they burned out, the whole tower would fall in.

Men with shovels attempted to smother the fire,

but in vain. The flames spread along the oakum-stuffed cracks, igniting more timbers. Colonel Roebling ordered men to smother the fire with carbonic gas, but the moment the workmen turned off the gas, the flames sprang up again. For the first time it was realized that under greatly increased air pressure you cannot blow out a flame.

Undismayed, Colonel Roebling directed his men to deluge the fire with two powerful hoses. After a

four-hour drenching the fire was out — or was it? Still
suspicious, Colonel Roebling had carpenters drill
holes through the first two courses of timbers to make
certain. No fire was found. But still apprehensive
four hours later, Colonel Roebling ordered them to
bore a four-foot hole. And the hole revealed that the
entire fourth layer of timbers was alive and glowing!

Now desperate, Colonel Roebling had to do some-
thing quickly even if it meant another kind of damage
to the caisson. Ordering the men out, he called

the Brooklyn fire department. Pumping engines on barges, a harbor fireboat, and two tugboats for five hours poured more than a million gallons of water into the caisson. Roebling left the underwater chamber flooded for two and a half days. That put out the fire!

The fire was caused accidentally. Edison had not yet invented the electric lightbulb, and the diggers worked by gas lamps and candles. A workman looking for his lunch in a dark corner had held his candle too close to a bit of highly inflammable oakum in the ceiling. The air pressure had driven the flame into the wood out of sight, and it was not discovered until the first course of timber in the ceiling had burned through.

When the water was pumped out of the caisson, it was found to be undamaged except for the burned timbers. Whereupon Colonel Roebling turned dentist and had the burned sections cleaned out like cavities in teeth. Then he had them filled with concrete.

Two weeks after the great fire the giant's foot reached rocky bottom. There was no need to go deeper. The caisson was packed with concrete, and there it stands today, forty-four feet down, surrounded by ooze and sand, supporting a mammoth tower rising hundreds of feet in the air.

If the Brooklyn tower presented difficult problems, constructing the giant's New York foot was a truly gigantic task, for men in this caisson had to dig nearly twice as deep to reach solid bottom. One year after the Brooklyn caisson was placed in starting position the New York caisson was towed to its site. The top of this shell was twenty-two feet thick, since it had to carry a much greater weight of stone than the other. To guard against fire, the ceiling and inside walls were covered with sheet metal.

All went well until the caisson neared its final resting place. Then the air pressure needed to keep the East River out became so great — thirty-five pounds to the square inch (normal air pressure is fifteen pounds) — that even the strongest men could work no longer than two hours at a time. In the caisson, men lost their sense of smell, and coming out of it they were attacked

by the bends, for science had not yet discovered that air pressure must be lowered very gradually to avoid this dread reaction.

As the disaster threatened, Colonel Roebling hastened to forestall them, spending whole days and nights in the caisson like a general on the battlefield. Even his great strength and endurance could not stand the strain of the frequent changes of air pressure that had already killed several workmen. One day when the New York caisson was well down, he was stricken so badly that he was carried, partially paralyzed, half blind, and half deaf, to his home in Brooklyn, to be an invalid for the rest of his life. Even then he refused to give in. The bridge had to be finished.

When Colonel Roebling recovered from the first shock, he sat in a chair in a room on the top floor of his home and through a pair of powerful binoculars kept track of the progress of the work. His wife was his assistant. Emily Warren Roebling, like her husband, was a remarkable person. The sister of Colonel Roebling's commanding general in the Civil War, she quickly learned enough engineering to explain her husband's plans and orders to his engineers.

The New York tower was finished in July, 1876, one year after the Brooklyn tower. The giant now had feet and legs; it needed a body and arms. To support the highway which was the bridge itself human spiders would spin their webs of steel.

Anchored firmly in a stone platform on the New York side, four thick cables were to swing up to the top of the New York tower, loop gracefully down to touch the completed highway over the middle of the

45

East River, climb to the top of the Brooklyn tower, and then drop to be anchored in another massive abutment. Smaller cables descending from the main cables would hold up all parts of the highway.

Before starting the main cables Colonel Roebling ordered a smaller trial cable hung from shore to shore over the tops of the two towers to guide the cable spinners and riggers in their work. Standing on the dizzy height of the Brooklyn tower, the workmen followed with their eyes the long loop of this cable as it hung far above the 1600 feet of water separating the two towers. The thought of working out over this abyss was too much. They refused to go on with the job.

Frank Farrington, chief mechanic, tried to calm the fears of the riggers but the more he pleaded, the more terrified they became. Then, to show that there was nothing to be afraid of, Farrington announced that on the following day he himself would cross on the cable in a "bosun's chair." News of this projected journey reached the newspapers, and all New York City and Brooklyn were electrified by the thought of the daring ride.

Nearly a half million people turned out for this

greatest trapeze act of all time. Every rooftop within binocular sight of the two towers was crammed with people, thousands jammed the streets of the waterfronts, and more thousands crowded into every available boat and ferry to gaze up with awe at the tiny thread of cable on which a man was to risk his life. "Will Farrington make it?" was the question on everyone's lips, and there were plenty of people who wagered money that he would go to his death.

A bosun's chair is a seat dangling from a wheel which runs on an overhead line. Ropes are attached to the front and back of the seat so that it may be pulled in either direction. Every ship carries at least one bosun's chair. It is used to cross from ship to ship in the open sea when it is too rough to launch a small boat. The chairs are rigged also to rescue people from sinking ships. The cable on which Farrington's chair rode was really an endless "traveler" wire only three-quarters of an inch thick. The wire was moved by a stationary engine at the Brooklyn anchorage.

Farrington calmly took his place in the bosun's chair, flashed a big smile as if he were going on a roller-coaster ride, lighted his pipe, and gave the signal for the start. As cannon boomed and excited thousands cheered, the tiny chair began its ascent from the abutment to the Brooklyn tower. To those at a distance the cable was invisible and the tiny speck that was Farrington seemed to be riding on thin air. Workers carried him over the top of the tower and launched him across the great reach.

Farrington gained the New York tower safely and a crew there carried him over its top and sent him on his last lap to the shore abutment. As he got out of his chair and waved his handkerchief in salute, the roar of the people was louder than the thundering of cannon and the blasting of steam whistles. The great spectacle was over and the riggers' fears were ended. The cable stringing could start.

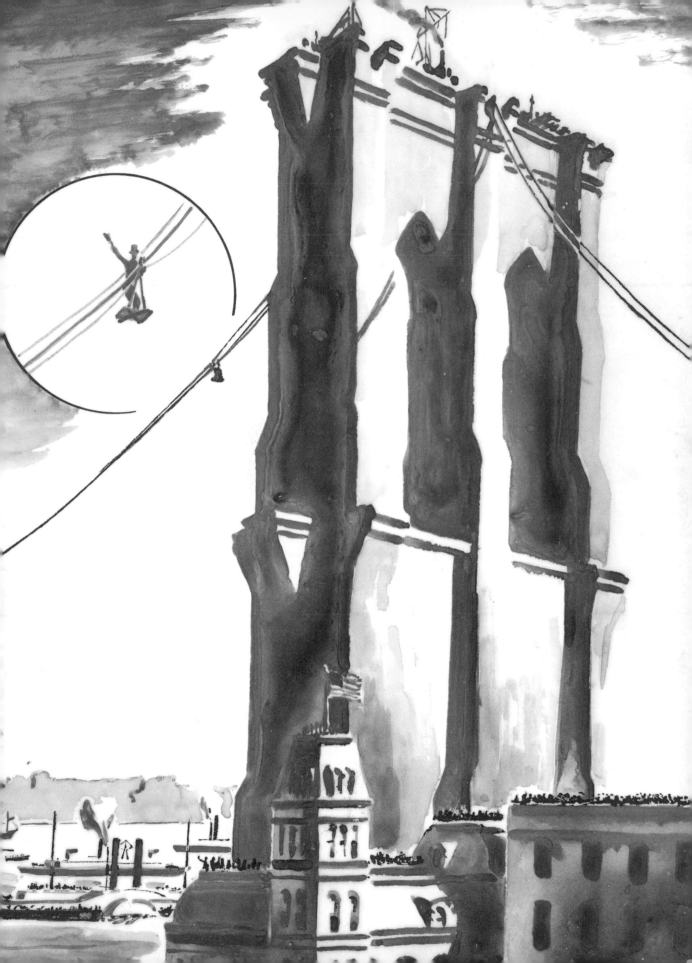

A cable is based on the idea that many strands of steel wire tied together in a single metal rope is many times stronger than the same thickness of steel in a solid piece. Colonel Roebling's father had perfected this idea and he had a factory in New Jersey to make steel wire and cables.

Although they may not look it, the four main

cables, the giant's arms, are very heavy. Nearly sixteen inches in diameter, they were too big to make at the factory and handle in the tremendous lengths needed. Riggers built them, high up in the air over the river, putting them together strand by strand until hundreds of wires in parallel lines were encased in a shell of watertight lead to keep them from rusting. The spinners worked on swaying catwalks that sometimes swung dangerously in a stiff breeze. There were no casualties among the riggers, but there were some near-fatal accidents to spectators, who got passes from the management to walk the catwalks despite Colonel Roebling's disapproval. Occasionally a spectator would get part way across the river on the swinging footbridges, look down, and freeze with fear. When that happened, a rigger would have to leave his work and lead the shaking visitor back to safety.

Then, as a completed cable was being anchored at one end, it tore loose from the abutment. Like a mighty whip it lashed through the air, grazing house-tops. It flicked out the lives of two workmen, and thrashed the East River like a snake in its death agonies. Luckily no ships or ferries were passing be-

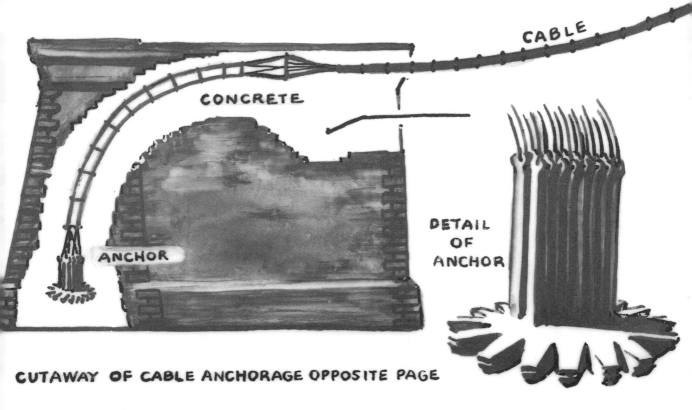

CABLE

CONCRETE

ANCHOR

DETAIL OF ANCHOR

CUTAWAY OF CABLE ANCHORAGE OPPOSITE PAGE

neath the cables at the time, or the toll would have been much heavier. An excursion boat that had carried people out to look at the growing giant had just left the area.

When the four main cables were completed, riggers dropped the smaller cables downward from them to support the roadway. This was put together section by section, first from the shore abutments to the towers and then out from the towers to meet in the middle. All of the three great sections of roadway arch a little in their centers for greater strength.

It took fourteen years to build the grandfather of great suspension bridges, but at last in 1883 it stood complete, rising from the East River as if conjured up from the depths by magicians, inviting the people of two great communities to come together.

Never before or since has there been such a bridge-opening celebration. People went wild with joy. Bands played. Politicians made speeches. Ships decorated with bunting and flags sailed gaily under the central span, tooting and blasting their whistles. At night fireworks burst and split the sky in all combinations of color. The President of the United States, Chester A. Arthur, was there to cut the ribbon officially opening the giant to traffic. At last the people

of Brooklyn and Long Island were free to come and go as they liked. No more waiting for ferries, no more dangerous crossings, and no more losing a day's pay because one could not cross at all!

But after the celebration the bridge was again involved in sickening tragedy. A hundred thousand people had walked safely over the bridge on the opening day. Yet six days later a man in the middle of the great span far above the river looked up at the delicate network of cables supporting him, became panic-

stricken and began to shout that the bridge was going to fall. Screaming in terror, the hundreds on the bridge ran for the exits. Many stumbled and fell, but those behind them never stopped. They trampled the fallen, killing and maiming as they ran to escape. When the last person had left the bridge, the survivors looked back. The bridge was still standing! But twelve people lay dead and forty more were badly injured.

There were three ways to cross the bridge: on foot

using a cross walk in the center; by a cable car, a kind
of railway car hauled back and forth by a cable attached to the car and carried between the tracks; or in
carriages, carts and wagons, using the roadways following the outside edges.

At first those who crossed had to pay to use Brooklyn Bridge because private individuals had put up the
money to build the giant, and they wanted to get their
money back and make some, too. But the people of
Brooklyn did not mind paying. If you have lived on an
island and have been forced to stay there many times
when you wanted to cross to the mainland, you can

understand that it is worth a great deal to be able to go to the city across the river any time you wish.

The fame of the giant spread. People came from all over the United States and from many foreign countries to see this seventh wonder of the world. They marveled as they looked up at the lofty double-arched towers rising above them. They were thrilled as they walked on the cross walk, watching oceangoing ships pass below. They were fascinated by the skylines of the two cities, and they were amazed at the lacy web that held the highway with its constantly changing loads.

So great was the fame of the bridge that there were those who tried to win fame for themselves by doing stunts on the bridge. Some, like Steve Brodie, went to their deaths. Brodie thought he could jump from the middle of the long span and dive into the water below. But jumping into water from such a great height is almost like landing on concrete. Brodie was killed but he did win a kind of fame, because for a long time men used the expression "He took a chance like Steve Brodie!"

More and more people came to Brooklyn and Long Island to live because they could easily get to work in

New York. Soon even the giant could not handle all the traffic. So twenty-five years later two other giants stood near Brooklyn Bridge with their feet in the East River: Williamsburg Bridge and Manhattan Bridge. They were built like the first except that their towers were made of structural steel, which had just been invented and which could be put together much more quickly than stones could be laid one on top of another.

There are longer suspension bridges, now, and quicker ways of building them, but Brooklyn Bridge has grandeur and beauty surpassing any other giant suspension bridge, for the man who designed it was more than an engineer; he was an artist. More than any other bridge it freed man's thoughts. It was the bridge that could not be built. When it was built after all, bridges began to appear in even more impossible places than the East River.

Brooklyn Bridge with its companions made metropolitan New York the largest city in the world. But best of all the giant set the people of Brooklyn free, and the spirit of Brooklyn Bridge has gone on setting people free all over the world.

The next time you are in New York, walk across

the giant, and you will begin to feel its grandeur and to understand why artists and authors have painted and written more about this bridge than all other bridges put together. Even though it is over eighty years old Brooklyn Bridge is still strong, useful, handsome, and inspiring!

INDEX